Woodland Fairy

Tooth Fairy

Water Fairy

Fairy Godmother

Starbright

Toadstool Fairy

corn fairy

fairy Queen

flower fairy

Moonbeam

Christmas Fairy

Buttercup

Flutter

Seaspray

Rainbow Fairy　　Sunshine Fairy

Puddle

Whoosh

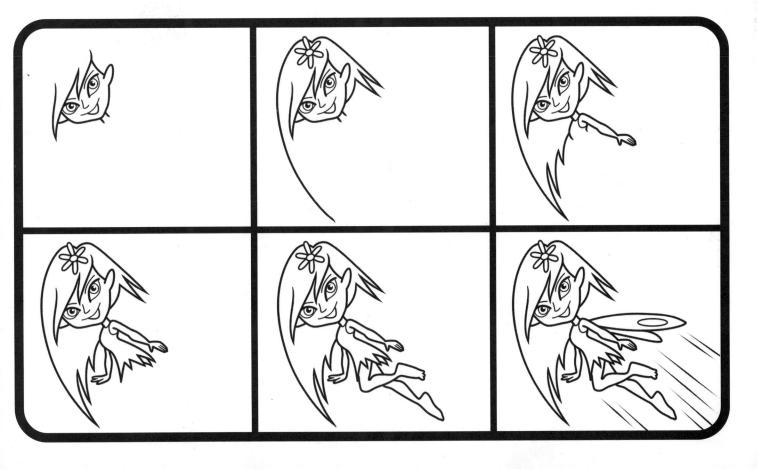

Glitter

Trixie

Velvet

Snoozy

Ruby

Daisy

Blink

Sparkle

Bubbles

Firefly

Emerald

Dewdrop

Hiccup   Breeze

Dimples

Fluffy

Blush

Freckles

Rose

Snowdrop

Beauty

Loveheart

Twizzle

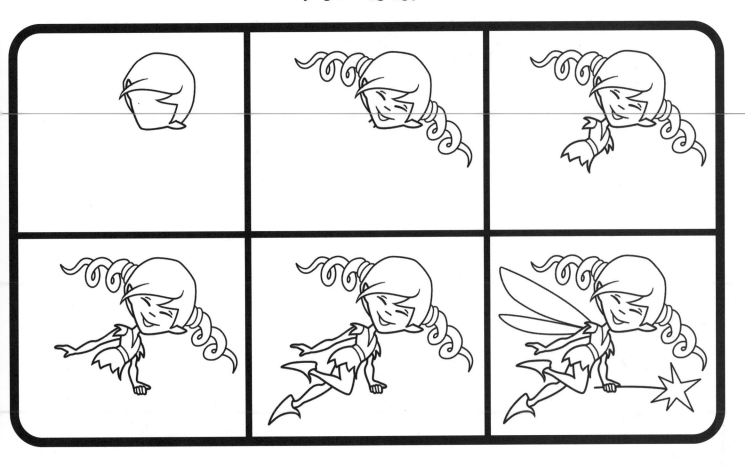

Sapphire

Dazzle

Misty

Dizzy

Lollipop

Candy

fizz

Goldie

Charm

Snowflake

Jester

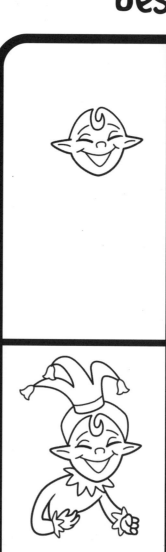

Whistler

Smudge

crystal

Tiny

Sunflower

Fidget

chuckles   cuddles

Lotus

Bumble

Shuffle

Jasmine

Raven

Alpine

Blossom   Ariel

Snuggles

Minty

Tulip

Amble

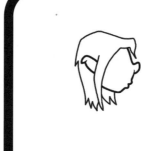

cupcake

Seashell

Prancer

Willow

flash

flora

Hazel

Pebble

frazzle

Hawkwind

Pinky

Butterscotch

Venus

Jacaranda

Nibs

Cherry

Violet

Grace

Nixie

Coral

Andromeda

Petunia

Dragonfly

Baubles

Nightingale

Indigo

Elfin

Jiggle

Melody